D1030526

A BEACON ❀ BIOGRAPHY

Angelina
JOLIE

Kayleen Reusser

PURPLE TOAD
PUBLISHING

Copyright © 2016 by Purple Toad Publishing, Inc. All rights reserved. No part of this book may be reproduced without written permission from the publisher. Printed and bound in the United States of America.

Printing   1   2   3   4   5   6   7   8   9

A Beacon Biography

Angelina Jolie
Big Time Rush
Carly Rae Jepsen
Drake
Ed Sheeran
Harry Styles of One Direction
Jennifer Lawrence
Kevin Durant
Lorde
Malala
Markus "Notch" Persson, Creator of Minecraft
Mo'ne Davis
Muhammad Ali
Neil deGrasse Tyson
Peyton Manning
Robert Griffin III (RG3)

Publisher's Cataloging-in-Publication Data
Reusser, Kayleen.
    Angelina Jolie / written by Kayleen Reusser.
        p. cm.
                Includes bibliographic references and index.
                ISBN 9781624691850
1. Jolie, Angelina, 1975—Juvenile literature. 2. Motion picture actors and actresses—United States—Biography—Juvenile literature. I. Series: Beacon Biographies Collection Two.
    PN2287 2016
    791.4302/8092

                                    Library of Congress Control Number: 2015941813

eBook ISBN: 9781624691867

ABOUT THE AUTHOR: Kayleen Reusser is author of a dozen children's books. She lives in Indiana and travels all over the country speaking to children and other groups about the craft of writing. Find out more at www.KayleenR.com.

PUBLISHER'S NOTE: The data in this book has been researched in depth, and to the best of our knowledge is factual. Although every measure is taken to give an accurate account, Purple Toad Publishing makes no warranty of the accuracy of the information and is not liable for damages caused by inaccuracies. This story has not been authorized or endorsed by Angelina Jolie.

CONTENTS

Angelina Jolie turns dreams into reality. She helps people around the world live better lives.

Angelina Jolie looked around. She stood on a grassy strip with tall trees nearby. Several women surrounded her, but Jolie didn't see anyone she knew. She rubbed the back of her neck with her hand. Both were dirty. The women looked as tired and dusty as Jolie felt. The sun beat down, making her skin prickly with heat. She was hungry and thirsty, but there was no food or water in sight.

Jolie tried to stay calm. *Where am I?* she wondered. *What has happened to me?*

She tried to remember what had brought her to this place. She knew she was an American actress who lived in Los Angeles. She was wealthy and owned several homes. She had won a number of awards for her acting ability.

While making the movie, *Lara Croft: Tomb Raider* in Cambodia in 2001, Jolie had noticed the poverty of many of the people who lived there. They didn't have nice homes or much food. Yet, they were kind and gracious.

Lara Croft: Tomb Raider became a worldwide sensation. Jolie was more popular than she had ever been in her life. But she had left the country with more on her mind than popularity.

After filming was completed, she returned to the United States, determined to aid people like those she had met in Cambodia.

Jolie contacted the United Nations High Commissioner for Refugees (UNHCR). This group traveled around the world assisting people in need. "Could I go with you on one trip to learn what I can do to help people?" Jolie asked. She insisted on paying her expenses and being treated like everyone else. The UNHCR agreed.

On February 22, 2001, Jolie accompanied the UNHCR to Sierra Leone and Tanzania in Africa. Parts of the trip were frightening. Army helicopters hovered at the airport. Broken glass was stuck to the top of cement walls surrounding the building where she stayed with other UNHCR workers. A guard patrolled the gate of the house.

Jolie tried to calm herself. Peeking around the heads of women waiting patiently in line, she saw papers covering a table. People wearing uniforms sat at the table talking to the women. *Are the people in uniform from the government?* she asked herself.

Jolie had heard stories about people running from government authorities and being attacked. Other people had escaped to start a new life with only bundles on their backs.

She gasped. She suddenly knew where she was. She and the other women were in line at a checkpoint for Internally Displaced Persons (IDPs). These were people who had been forced to leave their homes with nowhere to go.

Jolie had learned IDPs needed schools and food. As she stood in line with the other women, she began to understand how it must feel to have no home. She would have to go where the people with all of the papers told her to go.

Suddenly, Jolie woke up. It was a dream! She remembered that she was no longer in Cambodia. She had traveled to Africa on a second trip with UNHCR. Even though she knew the dream wasn't real, she was shaken by it.

The dream helped Jolie focus on the people around her in Sierra Leone and Tanzania. For the next two weeks, she learned much about their needs. The information was startling.

Jolie meets the displaced

- More than 20 million people in the world are IDPs or refugees.
- One-sixth of the world's population lives on less than one dollar a day.
- 1 billion people do not have safe drinking water.
- One-third of the world has no electricity.
- More than 100 million children are not in school.
- One in six children in Africa dies before the age of five.

When Jolie flew home from Africa, she returned to a greatly different life in Los Angeles. Her large home was luxurious and safe. She had food to eat and friends to see. She earned much money as an actress. Jolie was happily married to another actor, Billy Bob Thornton. She had good relationships with her mother and brother.

Still, Jolie could not forget the people she had met in Africa. She told people in Los Angeles that she planned to do more to help poor people around the world.

Some people doubted if Angelina Jolie, a busy actress who had several movies yet to make, would stay interested in helping poor people half a world away.

Jolie would prove them wrong.

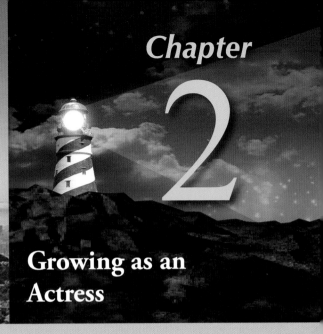

Top: Jolie's parents, actor Jon Voigt and Marcheline Bertrand.
Left: Angelina was born in Los Angeles, California (background).
Right: Jolie starred in her first movie, **Lookin' to Get Out,** at age eight with her father.
Bottom: Jolie began modeling at age 14.

Growing as an Actress

Jolie was born on June 4, 1975, in Los Angeles. Her father is actor Jon Voigt. He and her mother, Marcheline Bertrand, separated when Jolie was just a toddler. Her only sibling, an older brother named James, was born in 1973.

Jolie and James lived with their mother after their parents divorced in 1980. Jolie saw her father often as she grew up. He attended her soccer games. She accompanied him to movie premieres.

When she was seven years old, Jolie made her film debut. In *Lookin' to Get Out,* she played the part of Voigt's character's daughter.

Jolie attended El Rodeo School in Beverly Hills. With braces and a thin body, she was often made fun of. Jolie didn't let mean remarks stop her. She played soccer and took ballet and piano lessons. She was also involved in the school drama program.

As a child, Jolie didn't think of acting as a career. Instead, she began modeling at age fourteen. But, after earning a certificate from Morena High School, she enrolled in the Lee Strasberg Institute in New York. It was an acting school for people who wanted to be successful on stage or on screen. Jolie's mother had studied there.

For two years, Jolie focused on her acting career. She spent little time with friends. Instead, she went to acting classes and hundreds of auditions. She worked hard at lessons in fencing, boxing, and ballroom dancing—skills she thought she might need as an actress.

It was not easy. One of her early acting roles was a talking salamander. Jolie refused to give up.

Jolie's father had friends who worked in movies. If she had mentioned who her father was to them, they might have given her a part. But she refused to tell anyone who she was related to. She changed her name from Angelina Jolie Voigt to simply Angelina Jolie. She wanted to earn acting jobs based on her own skills.

Eventually, directors noticed her natural acting talent and willingness to work hard. She was hired to act in small movie roles. Like most people, Jolie's skills as an actress improved with experience.

In 1998, she won a Golden Globe Award as the wife of a famous southern governor in the film *George Wallace.* In 1999, she won an Oscar for Best Supporting Actress playing a woman in a mental institution in *Girl, Interrupted.*

While the awards made her famous in the United States, a different movie made her famous around the world—*Lara Croft: Tomb Raider.*

Lara Croft is a character in a popular video game and comic book. The first time Jolie was offered the movie role, she turned it down. She had tried to play the video game and didn't like it. When the director asked her a second time to portray Lara Croft, Jolie agreed.

In the movie, Lara Croft is an archeologist and photojournalist from England. She leads an exciting life, swinging from the rafters of her British

Jolie in **Girl, interrupted**

Jolie as Lara Croft

mansion, running through jungles, and fighting enemies.

Some actresses would have asked for a stunt double to perform the risky scenes. Not Jolie. "I always wanted to be Indiana Jones or James Bond," she said.

Filming the movie in Cambodia, one of the world's ten poorest countries, opened Jolie's eyes. It was her first exposure to how the world's poor people lived.

In July 2001, when she traveled to Cambodia with UNHCR, Jolie tried to learn as much as she could about how to assist the people there with basic needs like food and water. She was overwhelmed by their courage. "There is a kindness they showed to me and to each other—a softness and a sadness. They have all been witness to the worst

suffering in the world. They know loss and death, but they also know the value of friendship and hope," she wrote in her journal.

Jolie was deeply inspired by the people of Cambodia. She would soon realize how the trip there would change her life forever.

In Cambodia with UNHCR

In Cambodia Jolie worked with children, many of whom had no school or place to live.

Caring for Cambodia

Jolie had fallen in love with Cambodia while filming the movie *Lara Croft: Tomb Raider.* She knew as an actress she had a unique opportunity to reach out to the people there with assistance. "If I can use this celebrity thing in a positive way, that will be worth it," she said.

Three special things happened to Jolie in Cambodia that would change her life.

In the 1970s, Cambodia had been involved in a war. Soldiers had buried thousands of land mines. These explosives are very hard to see. Stepping on one can be fatal—for the person who triggered it and for anyone nearby.

Fifty percent of land mine victims die, either at the moment of explosion or from bleeding to death. The 50 percent who survive are nearly all amputees.

Someone translated a song for Jolie that Cambodian children sang. The lyrics began with a description about how beautiful their country was. It ended with a warning: "If we see one (land mine), don't touch it."

When Jolie heard the children singing about the dangers of land mines, she wanted to do something about it.

Jolie helps destroy a land mine

She joined a group that cleared land mines and other types of explosives in Cambodia. One of Jolie's favorite moments of the trip was being allowed to safely detonate a land mine. "It was a great feeling to destroy something that would have otherwise hurt or possibly killed another person," she wrote in her journal.

The second thing that made Jolie happy was when the UNHCR asked her to be a Goodwill Ambassador. On her first trip to Sierra Leone and Tanzania, she had participated as a volunteer.

As an ambassador, Jolie knew she would meet more people and be responsible for sharing information in discussions. She still had much to learn about the needs of people who lived in struggling areas. Jolie was willing to invest the time and effort. "I can't express how happy and honored I was to be made an ambassador for UNHCR," she wrote.

Jolie watched other UNHCR volunteers for inspiration on how best to fulfill her duties as ambassador. "Everyone with UNHCR puts themselves in danger," she wrote in her journal. "Not only do these aid workers never complain about the difficulties, but they say they feel lucky to help."

Detonating a land mine to save lives in Cambodia had thrilled Jolie. But being appointed an ambassador with UNHCR filled her with purpose. She hoped to learn more as an ambassador to help children and adults around the world.

"The world is a lot bigger than I thought it was," she wrote after visiting Cambodia. "There is a lot I have to learn. I didn't know what that country had gone through. The people were so warm and beautiful and pure and honest. I just loved the country."

In 2002, Jolie again traveled with UNHCR, this time to Ecuador. She kept a journal of her thoughts and experiences. So many people wanted to read her notes about traveling with UNHCR that Jolie put them into a book—*Notes from My Travels*.

Helping people around the world inspired her, but she still had a busy life in Los Angeles. At 25 years old, she had a steady career as an actress. She had won awards for her acting ability. Paparazzi intruded on her privacy with husband, Billy Bob Thornton. He and Jolie had married in 2000.

Jolie had learned to handle the media's attention on her every move. She was considered one of the world's most beautiful women, and people wanted to see her dressed in glamorous gowns for special parties and award ceremonies.

Her trips with UNHCR had changed her. In the past, she might stay at a party all night or get a tattoo. Now, Jolie wanted to focus on helping people in need.

She also made a choice to change her life in a way that shocked people who knew her. Some people might have hesitated, but Jolie knew it was the right decision for her. She would adopt a baby from Cambodia.

When the public found out about her interest in adopting a baby, they wanted to know—would Angelina Jolie be a good mother?

Jolie meets the people of Ecuador

Angelina Jolie adopted a baby boy from a Cambodian orphanage. She named him Maddox.

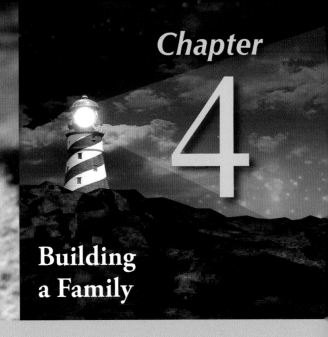

In 2003, when Jolie learned that hunters were poaching endangered animals in a national park in Cambodia, she bought 150,000 acres of the park. She made it the Maddox Jolie Project, a wildlife reserve named after her son. Animals like the clouded leopard now have a safer place to live.

Building a Family

Jolie's parents had divorced when she was young. With a challenging home life and a busy film career she had had little interest in becoming a mother.

After seeing so many children in need in Cambodia, Jolie was determined to help one by adoption. She visited several orphanages in the country. Eventually, she found a baby boy living in Battambang, Cambodia's second largest city. Jolie named him Maddox Chivan, "Mad" for short. Mad was seven months old when she adopted him in March 2002.

Jolie happily told everyone she was ready to be a loving mother to Mad. "He is my life," she said. "I want to be a great parent. There was a time when I lived through my characters. I've now found that I prefer my life."

Unfortunately, Jolie's relationship with her husband suffered after the adoption. Billy Bob Thornton had a career and children of his own from a previous marriage. He and Jolie seemed to love each other deeply, yet they spent little time together after Maddox's adoption. The couple divorced in 2003.

(Thornton was Jolie's second husband. She had married British actor, Jonny Lee Miller, in 1996, and they divorced in 1999.)

In 2003, Jolie took Maddox with her to England to film the sequel *Lara Croft Tomb Raider: The Cradle of Life.* Jolie liked living in England so much that she bought a home there for her and Maddox. She also owned homes in Los Angeles and New York City.

With her adoption of Maddox, Jolie's goals seemed focused. She continued her travels for UNHCR, visiting Sri Lanka, Jordan, Egypt, Kosovo, and Lebanon, among others. Her brother, James, often accompanied her on trips.

Jolie contributed millions of dollars to helping children and adults by building orphanages and shipping school supplies and food around the world.

In 2002, the Angelina Jolie Primary School was set up in Kenya by the UNHCR to educate young girls.

In addition to providing food and water to displaced people in Kenya, Jolie set up a school for girls.

People thanked Jolie for her help. In October 2003, she was awarded the first Citizen of the World Award by the United Nations Correspondents Association. Secretary General Kofi Annan presented the award, which "brings public attention to the plight of refugees across the globe so the world community will take action to help them."

Jolie was thrilled with the award. "It means I've done good work for an organization that I care about a great deal and that I didn't let them down," she

Jolie speaks after accepting the Citizen of the World Award.

said. "If I die tomorrow, I can leave my son something that says I did something good with my life."

In 2005, she created the National Center for Refugee and Immigrant Children. This organization provides legal assistance to the youngest refugees. Jolie gave it an endowment of $2 million to help it continue its work.

That same year, Jolie's life changed again when she starred in the movie *Mr. and Mrs. Smith*. Her costar was another famous actor, Brad Pitt. He had starred in many films including *Ocean's Eleven* and *Troy*.

Pitt, like Jolie, was concerned for people in crisis. In 2005, he organized a housing project to rebuild neighborhoods destroyed by

Jolie and Pitt have their own acting and directing careers, but they make time to take part in humanitarian events around the world together.

Hurricane Katrina. He also founded Not On Our Watch, an organization that worked against genocide.

Jolie and Pitt fell in love. During the next few years, the couple adopted two more children and had three of their own. Zahara Marley was born in Ethiopia in 2005 and adopted later that year by Jolie and Pitt. Pax Thien was born in Vietnam in 2003 and adopted by Jolie in 2007.

Shiloh Nouvel Jolie-Pitt was the couple's first biological child. She was born May 27, 2006, in Namibia, a country in Africa. On July 12, 2008, Angelina gave birth to twins, Knox Leon and Vivienne Marcheline Jolie-Pitt, in France.

Angelina Jolie wanted to honor the countries where her adopted children were born. She bought 21 acres of land in Cambodia for Mad. "I want him to know his language and his people," she said. In 2005, she helped fund a pediatric AIDS clinic in Ethiopia.

She continued to win awards for her acting, including an Oscar and three Golden Globe awards.

In the midst of this happy time in Jolie's life, her mother died. Marcheline Bertrand had suffered from ovarian cancer for seven years. She passed away on January 27, 2007, with family at her side. Jolie was relieved Marcheline was no longer in pain from the illness, but she missed her dearly.

As the mother of a large family of young children, with a busy film career, loving partner, and humanitarian duties, Jolie was busier than ever. People wondered if she could continue to balance it all. Would Angelina Jolie need to make some changes in her life?

Jolie and partner Brad Pitt often travel with their six children.

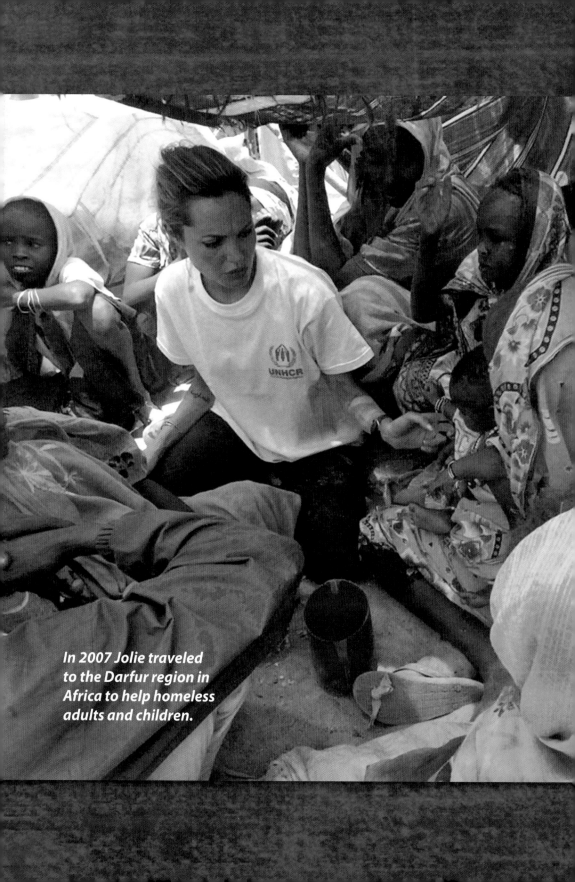

In 2007 Jolie traveled to the Darfur region in Africa to help homeless adults and children.

Helping
the World

With Pitt's partnership, Jolie's humanitarian work seemed unstoppable. In 2006, the couple formed the Jolie-Pitt Foundation, a charity to aid the four million people affected by the war in Darfur. After Jolie visited Darfur in February 2007, the Jolie-Pitts donated $1 million to the charity.

In 2007, Jolie became a member of the Council on Foreign Relations. The next year, she helped found Kids in Need of Defense (KIND). This was another organization designed to help refugee children in the United States with legal problems.

After the earthquake in Haiti in 2010, the Jolie-Pitts donated $1 million to the group Doctors Without Borders. Jolie visited Haiti to see the progress made by relief efforts. The Jolie-Pitts gave several million dollars to other charities around the world as well.

Jolie received more recognition for her humanitarian efforts. In 2011, the UNHCR honored her for 10 years of service.

In 2014, she received the Jean Hersholt Humanitarian Award. She was also asked to serve another term as a United Nations (UN) Goodwill Ambassador.

For years, Jolie had worked with London's government to establish a place that taught women how to stay safe in war zones. England was grateful for Jolie's interest in educating its citizens. In 2015, Queen Elizabeth of England honored Jolie by making her an honorary dame.

Jolie discovered she wanted to use her skills as a director to show the challenges people experience. In 2007, she directed her first movie, the documentary *A Place in Time*. Jolie discovered she wanted to use her skills as a director to show the challenges people experience. She followed that in 2011 with *In the Land of Blood and Honey* about the Bosnian war.

In 2014, Jolie directed her biggest movie yet. *Unbroken* told the story of Louis Zamperini as he went from being an American Olympic runner to a World War II airman. Zamperini was captured by the Japanese and tortured before gaining freedom when the war

Jolie with former Foreign Secretary William Hague at the launch of a United Kingdom program to prevent violence, 2012

During World War II, Capt. Louis Zamperini (left) spent 28 months in a Japanese prison camp. Following his rescue, he spoke to the American people on the radio. Zamperini lived to be 97 years old. He died in July 2014, just before the film's release.

ended. The story is based on the book *Unbroken*, by Laura Hillenbrand. Perhaps her interest in the airman stems from another of her passions: Jolie is an accomplished pilot.

As a mother, Jolie made the film *Unbroken* with a PG-13 rating so that young people could learn about Zamperini's incredible survival story.

"I want my children to know about men like Louie," she said at a press conference. "When they feel bad about themselves and think all is lost, they will know they've got something inside of them. A strong heart and indomitable will and unbreakable spirit exists in each one of us. It made me face every day and every challenge differently."

With her mother's death, Jolie doubled her efforts to show love to her own children. She starred in movies they could enjoy. She was the voice of Lola the Angelfish in the movie *Shark Tale* (2004) and Tigress in *Kung Fu Panda* (2008).

In August 2014, Jolie and Pitt cemented their relationship when they married in France. (They had already married legally in a secret ceremony in the United States). Jolie and Pitt asked their six children to help with the wedding. Maddox and Pax walked Jolie down the aisle. Zahara and Vivienne threw flower petals. Knox and Shiloh served as ring bearers. Jolie changed her last name and that of their six children to Jolie-Pitt.

Jolie starred in more hit films, including *Maleficent.* The children's movie tells the story behind the evil fairy in the fairy tale *Sleeping Beauty. Maleficent* was voted Favorite Movie and Favorite Family Movie at the 2014 People's Choice Awards. Vivienne Jolie-Pitt made her film debut as young Princess Aurora.

Jolie continues to travel the world on behalf of people in need. She has visited Iraq five times since 2007. Her plans are to continue caring

Jolie starred in the movie **Maleficent,** *which puts a new spin on the tale* **Sleeping Beauty.**

Since 2007, Jolie has traveled to Iraq five times to help people in need.

for people in crisis. This is the same goal she had when she made her first visit to Africa in 2001.

"I honestly want to help," she wrote in her journal. "I don't believe I am different from other people. I think we all want justice and equality. We all want a chance for a life with meaning. All of us would like to believe that if we were in a bad situation someone would help us."

1975   Angelina Jolie is born on June 4.

1982   Jolie stars in her first movie, *Lookin' to Get Out,* with father Jon Voigt.

1989   Jolie begins modeling. She is cast in small movie parts.

1996   Jolie marries actor Jonny Lee Miller.

1998   Jolie wins a Golden Globe Award for the film *George Wallace.*

1999   Jolie wins Oscar Award for *Girl, Interrupted.* She divorces Miller.

2000   Jolie marries actor Billy Bob Thornton.

2001   *Lara Croft: Tomb Raider* released. Jolie accompanies UNHCR to Sierra Leone and Tanzania in Africa. UNHCR asks her to be a Goodwill Ambassador.

2002   Jolie goes to Ecuador with UNHCR. She adopts Maddox Chivan, an infant from Cambodia. She establishes the Angelina Jolie Primary School in Kenya.

2003   Jolie divorces Thornton. She receives the first Citizen of the World Award from the United Nations Correspondents Association.

2005   Jolie creates the National Center for Refugee and Immigrant Children. Jolie stars in the movie *Mr. and Mrs. Smith* and begins relationship with co-star Brad Pitt. They adopt a daughter, Zahara Marley, from Ethiopia. Jolie helps fund a pediatric AIDS clinic in Ethiopia. She founds the National Center for Refugee and Immigrant Children.

2006   Shiloh Nouvel Jolie-Pitt, the couple's first biological child, is born in Namibia, a country in Africa. Jolie and Pitt form the Jolie-Pitt Foundation.

2007   Jolie adopts a son, Pax Thien, from Vietnam. Marcheline Bertrand, Jolie's mother, dies from ovarian cancer. Jolie becomes a member of the Council on Foreign Relations. She directs her first movie, the documentary *A Place in Time.* She begins a series of five trips to Iraq.

2008   Jolie gives birth to twins, Knox Leon and Vivienne Marcheline Jolie-Pitt, in France. She helps found Kids in Need of Defense (KIND). She is nominated for an Academy Award for Best Actress in *The Changeling.*

2010   The Jolie-Pitts donate $1 million to the group Doctors Without Borders.

2011   The UNHCR honors Jolie for 10 years of service. She directs *In the Land of Blood and Honey* about the Bosnian war.

2014   Jolie receives the Jean Hersholt Humanitarian Award. She is asked to become a United Nations Goodwill Ambassador. She directs *Unbroken.* Jolie and Pitt marry in France with children taking part in the wedding. She stars in the hit film *Maleficent* which wins Favorite Movie and Favorite Family Movie at the 2014 People's Choice Awards.

2015   Queen Elizabeth of England honors Jolie by making her an honorary dame.

2015	By the Sea (Director and Actor)	2003	Lara Croft Tomb Raider: The Cradle of Life
2014	Unbroken (Director)	2002	Life or Something Like It
2014	Maleficent	2001	Original Sin
2011	In the Land of Blood and Honey (Director)	2001	Lara Croft: Tomb Raider
2011	Kung Fu Panda 2	2000	Gone in Sixty Seconds
2010	The Tourist	1999	Girl, Interrupted
2010	Salt	1999	The Bone Collector
2008	Wanted	1999	Pushing Tin
2008	Changeling	1998	Playing by Heart
2008	Kung Fu Panda	1998	Hell's Kitchen
2007	Beowulf	1998	Gia (TV Movie)
2007	A Mighty Heart	1997	Playing God
2006	The Good Shepherd	1997	George Wallace (TV Movie)
2005	Mr. & Mrs. Smith	1997	True Women (TV Movie)
2004	Alexander	1996	Mojave Moon
2004	The Fever	1996	Foxfire
2004	Sky Captain and the World of Tomorrow	1996	Love Is All There Is
2004	Shark Tale	1995	Hackers
2004	Taking Lives	1995	Without Evidence
2003	Beyond Borders	1982	Lookin' to Get Out

Books

Bjornlund, Lydia. *Modern Role Models: Angelina Jolie.* Mason Crest Publishers: Broomall, PA, 2009.

Halperin, Ian. *Brangelina.* Transit Publishing: Montreal, 2009.

Hibbert, Clare. *Celeb Movie Star.* Sea-to-Sea Publications: Mankato, MN, 2012.

Jolie, Angelina. *Notes from My Travels.* Pocket Books: New York, 2003.

Mercer, Rhona. *Angelina Jolie: The Biography.* John Blake Publishing: London, 2007.

Morton, Andrew. *Angelina: An Unauthorized Biography.* St. Martin's Press: New York, 2010.

Works Consulted

"Angelina Jolie." *Newsmakers.* Detroit: Gale, 2000. Web.
March 30, 2015.

"Angelina Jolie dazzles at London premiere of *Unbroken.*" *Telegraph Online,* November 26, 2014. Web. March 30, 2015.

"Angelina Jolie: I'd consider politics if I could make a difference." *Telegraph Online,* November 25, 2014. Web. March 30, 2015.

"Angelina Jolie Opening Centre on Women, Peace and Security in London." *World Entertainment News Network,* February 10, 2015. Web. March 30, 2015.

"Angelina Jolie says PG-13 rating for 'Unbroken' was very important to her." *UPI NewsTrack,* December 7, 2014. Web. March 30, 2015.

"Angelina Jolie says she and Brad Pitt married before France nuptials." *UPI NewsTrack,* January 9, 2015.

"Angelina Jolie: 'Unbroken Made Me a Better Person.'" *World Entertainment News Network,* December 27, 2014. Web. March 30, 2015.

On the Internet

Angelina Jolie Biography
    http://www.ajjolie.com/biography
Brad Pitt Biography
    http://www.biography.com/people/brad-pitt-9441989
Look to the Stars: The World of Celebrity Giving
    https://www.looktothestars.org/charity/jolie-pitt-foundation
SOS Children's Villages
    http://www.cs.mcgill.ca/~rwest/wikispeedia/wpcd/wp/j/Jolie_Pitt.htm
The UN Refugee Agency
    http://www.unhcr.org/cgi-bin/texis/vtx/home

abroad (uh-BROD)—In or to a foreign country or countries.

ambassador (am-BASS-uh-dur)—A person who represents one country and visits other countries.

audition (aw-DIH-shin)—A reading of a part for a role in a theatrical performance, such as a play, before a director.

compassion (kum-PASH-in)—A feeling of deep sympathy and sorrow for another who is stricken by misfortune.

debut (day-BYOO)—First public appearance.

detonate (DEH-tuh-nayt)—Explode or cause to explode.

documentary (dok-yoo-MEN-tuh-ree)—A movie presenting facts and information, especially about a political, historical, or social subject.

endowment (en-DOW-mint)—A gift or grant.

genocide (JEH-nuh-syde)—The mass killing of a national, racial, political, or cultural group.

humanitarian (hyoo-man-ih-TAYR-ee-in)—A person who works for the rights and freedoms of other people.

paparazzi (pah-puh-ROT-zee)—Photographers who specialize in taking photos of celebrities.

pediatric (pee-dee-AH-trik)—Branch of medicine concerned with the care of babies and children.

premiere (pre-MEER)—A first public performance of a play or film.

refugee (reh-fyoo-JEE)—A person who seeks shelter in a foreign country to avoid war or persecution.

sequel (SEE-kwool)—A movie or other published work that continues a story, usually by using the same characters.

stunt double—Someone who looks like the actor and plays the dangerous parts in a movie or show so that the actor does not get injured.

PHOTO CREDITS: P. 19—United Nations; p. 24—Foreign and Commonwealth; p. 25—National Archives; All other photos—cc-by-sa-2.0. Every measure has been taken to find all copyright holders of material used in this book. In the event any mistakes or omissions have happened within, attempts to correct them will be made in future editions of the book.

J B JOLIE
Reusser, Kayleen,
Angelina Jolie /
R2003960198 MILTON

ODC

Atlanta-Fulton Public Library